Change is in your hands. There are steps here that can help.

YOU CAN

OVERCOME

ANXIETY AND

DEPRESSION

LIFE CHANGING STRATEGIES TO GIVE YOU
A SENSE OF WELL-BEING THAT WON'T QUIT
AND HELP YOU WANT TO GET UP IN THE MORNING

Jill Beytebiere

Author of 'The Whole Life Makeover Series'

OTHER BOOKS BY JILL FROM 'THE WHOLE LIFE MAKEOVER SERIES'

LIFE TO THE FULLEST: The Ultimate Guide To Help You Design An Awesome Life, Fit In Travel, Find Your Life's Work, Create An Online Presence, And More

EXPLODE YOUR LIMITS: Time Management Strategies To Get You Beyond The Daily Grind, Help You Squeeze The Most Out Of Life, And Enable You To Accomplish Your Dreams

THE TRANSFORM YOUR BODY DIET: AKA: The 14 Step, Exercise To Fit Your Life, Trade Fat For Muscle, Boost That Metabolism, Do Better Than Keto, Flood Your Body With Nutrition And Still Indulge Once In A While Diet

STAY AFLOAT POST-CV: Stretch Your Dollar From Here To Timbuktu, Find A Side Hustle, Own A Home Free And Clear, Invest In The Best, And Still Have Money To Give (If The Stars All Line Up)

BRAND YOUR LIFE'S WORK: How To Make Your Dream Business, Create An Online Presence, Do It Local, Nail It With Your Copy, Advertise The Heck Out Of It, And Scale It To The Highest Heavens (*Disclaimer Inside)

RELATIONSHIP Rx: How To Develop Relationships Post-Covid, Reach The Hearts Of Your Loved Ones, Deal With Them When They're Being Impossible, And Dig Yourself Out Of The Doghouse When You've Messed Up (From Someone Who Has Done Some Digging)

YOU CAN

OVERCOME

ANXIETY AND

DEPRESSION

LIFE CHANGING STRATEGIES TO GIVE YOU
A SENSE OF WELL-BEING THAT WON'T QUIT
AND HELP YOU WANT TO GET UP IN THE MORNING

Jill Beytebiere

Life Building Media
Seattle, WA

First printing 2020

ISBN: 978-1-7349304-9-8

Cover photo by Chip Lanay on Pixabay

Come to my website for fun contests, freebies, life changing content and more: jillandyou.com

DEDICATION

This book is dedicated to someone I love very much who has struggled with depression.

TABLE OF CONTENTS

IF YOU ARE IN A CRISIS

If you're dealing with anxiety or depression there's help in this book. But sometimes we're in a moment of crisis. If that's you be sure to reach out to someone. **The National Suicide Prevention line is 1-800-273-8255.** You can also look on your phone for local numbers.

Or call 911 if it's urgent.

Trouble shared
is trouble halved.
-Lee Iacocca

WE'RE IN THIS TOGETHER

CHAPTER 1

We're In This Together

Life really hurts sometimes. **And whatever you're going through, I want you to know I am in this for you.**

I can't stand the thought of anyone suffering, so my brain is constantly on a track, trying to find solutions to help with life's troubles. It's just the way I'm wired.

And I'll admit, I've had plenty of troubles myself. I feel the pain of life on a regular basis, mixed in with all the good. The good weighs out, though, thankfully, in the end.

THERE ARE CONSTRUCTIVE THINGS WE CAN DO THAT HELP

I'll share with you strategies I've used and some I trust others have found helpful, that can get us through our hard times and help us make the best of our lives. There are constructive things we can do, and this book will give you tools to hopefully help get you on a better footing.

WE CAN'T SOLVE EVERYTHING BUT LET'S IMPROVE WHAT WE CAN

Life is complex.

I can't fix all my own problems, let alone yours, but there are things that can make a difference for you. If you put in some effort.

And if we find even a few things to help us hold on and give us breathing space, it's worth it.

I'D LOVE TO HEAR FROM YOU

There's something you can do for me, too.

If this book helps you at all I'd love if you'd send me a very short little email and let me know what has worked. You'd be helping me to know the effort was worthwhile.

You can email me at:

contactme@jillandyou.com

I'll be super happy to hear from you. If nothing else send me an emoji.

My website is:
jillandyou.com

Life is 10% what happens
to us and 90% how
we react to it.
-Dennis P. Kimbro

HEALING TAKES EFFORT BUT IT'S PARTLY IN YOUR HANDS

CHAPTER 2

Healing Takes Effort But It's Partly In Your Hands

Are you feeling weighed down by things going on in the world these days? Or by the troubles in your own life? **I know there days that feel like an uphill climb with a heavy backpack and sometimes it's hard to keep going.**

Don't give up, though. We'll go over things to try that can help you have peace, even with all the troubles going on around us.

A LITTLE BIT OF EFFORT CAN TRANSFORM YOUR LIFE

You'll have to do a tiny bit of heavy lifting, though.

Nothing too tough. Just a little effort. Like reading this book, even if it's just a chapter a day. And then trying to implement some of the things that can make a difference for you.

CHANGE IS IN YOUR HANDS

Sometimes we need a counsellor or therapist, **but still a lot of the actual work is in your own hands.**

In fact, some of the things I recommend in this book you almost have to do in order to get better.

GET A THERAPIST IF YOU NEED ONE

I'm not saying don't find a therapist. **They can be super helpful.** It often makes us feel better when someone listens to our problems.

So, if you think you need a licensed professional, by all means, look around for one that will be a good match.

USING THIS BOOK, ALSO, WILL HELP YOU GROW EXPONENTIALLY

But use this book, also, and you'll grow exponentially. **If you take these suggestions to heart it'll help you to be more healthy emotionally and more well-balanced, as well.** No matter what life throws at you.

Each lesson in here is like a puzzle piece. When you put it all together it can lead to a better picture. A better adjusted, and in many ways, happier you.

THE CHANGES YOU MAKE WILL ADD UP

Every change adds up. It keeps growing. **You'll feel good about the changes you make and that'll help you want to do more.**

It's like my mom said when I bought a new couch cover for my living room: "Once you make one change, you'll want to keep going. Next thing you know you'll have done the whole house."

It can go that way for you, too. You may have no idea what all you'll accomplish in life, once you get started.

Wherever you go, no matter what the weather, always bring your own sunshine.
-Anthony J. D'Angelo

DO YOUR THOUGHTS FEEL HEAVY?

(HERE'S HOW TO LIGHTEN THE LOAD...)

CHAPTER 3

Do Your Thoughts Feel Heavy? (Here's How To Lighten The Load...)

Do you ever feel like you can hardly breathe? Sometimes our thoughts are so heavy it feels like we are going to suffocate.

Coming up are some ways to rewire your brain to help wipe away anxiety and give you hope.

And that lifts the load, making our breathing easier.

STRAIGHTENING OUT OUR THOUGHTS HELPS US DE-STRESS

When you straighten your thoughts it'll combat stress. Even when it feels like troubles are breathing down your neck.

Some of these strategies can help you have peace even in the middle of a storm. They keep me buoyed when everything is falling apart around me. Usually.

Because life knocks me down, too, sometimes.

And it will be stressful now and then. No changing that. **But with your thoughts in line it'll be a lot easier to bounce back when life knocks you down.**

IT'S A CHOICE TO THINK BETTER THOUGHTS

Step one is to *decide* to think new thoughts.

You don't want to give up here and believe its hopeless.

It's a battle and to win you have to be willing to try.

At first it may be one of the toughest battles you face. You have to argue with those negative thoughts in your brain.

Kind of like playing ping pong. When a bad thought comes along you send back a hopeful one.

Sound tiring? It can be.

But it gets easier. Because eventually your brain stops arguing back quite as much. Good thoughts become more automatic.

ARE YOU READY TO REPLACE NEGATIVE THOUGHTS WITH POSITIVE ONES?

Do you feel ready to replace defeating thoughts with more positive ones?

I hope so. Because I can't get in there and do it for you. **But I completely trust you can win this one if you try.** Or at least make a huge dent in the problem.

HOW WE TALK IN OUR HEAD MATTERS

You might not realize it, but you are talking to yourself in your head all the time. And sometimes that talk can be pretty negative.

You can be your own worst enemy.

Thankfully, simply talking to yourself differently in your head can help change how you feel about life.

You just need to:

- Decide to replace bad thoughts
- Come up with a better thought when you catch yourself thinking defeating ones.

And in the next chapter I'll show you how it works.

The greatest discovery of all time is that a person can change his future by merely changing his attitude.
-Oprah Winfrey

CATCH THOSE
RATTY THOUGHTS

CHAPTER 4

Catch Those Ratty Thoughts

Sometimes the things we think defeat us.

It's important to stop and look at those thoughts once in a while and to catch the ones that stink. Like you might catch a rat.

This is the first step: Watch for and catch ratty thoughts. Then replace them with better ones.

SOME EXAMPLES OF REPLACEMENT THOUGHTS

Ask yourself which thought is better:

- "There's no hope." Or "There must be a solution."
- "Things are never going to get better." Or "Things will get better eventually."
- "I'm a failure." Or "Everyone makes mistakes."
- "This is terrible." Or "This is bad, but I'll get through it."
- "Life is awful." Or "Some days are tough but other days are better."
- "My life is worse than anyone else's." Or "Everyone has troubles. It's just part of life."
- "I can't take it anymore." Or "I'm going to hang in there. There will be easier days."
- "I'm good for nothing." Or "I have value. I matter."

You get the idea.

When we tell ourselves negative things it drains us of hope. It takes away our initiative. Kind of a self-fulfilling prophecy, if only because we don't try as hard.

IT'S HARD TO THINK POSITIVE WHEN WE HAVE TROUBLES

When you're feeling down it might seem impossible to change what's going on in your head.

But there's a little known secret that can turn things around for you...

You don't have to believe it.

Better thoughts are simply a decision to tell yourself good news.

"I'm going to think I'll make it through this, if it kills me," you can tell yourself through gritted teeth.

And usually, if we think new thoughts we end up believing them.

BUT WHAT IF THE NEGATIVE THOUGHTS ARE TRUE?

First of all, they're probably not. But even if they were, which thoughts are going to make you happier?

If you're wrong you're still better off, right? **You've got nothing to lose by thinking more positive.** And a whole lot to gain.

So, if you don't believe the positive thoughts, think them anyway. Because when you have hope things do get better to some degree.

I CAN'T PREDICT THE FUTURE, BUT...

I don't know what all is ahead for you, but no matter how positively we think life can turn out to be a nightmare, like during a war or the Holocaust.

Even then, though, we can try to make the best of it.

Corrie Ten Boom is a good example of seeing beyond your circumstances when going through horrifying times. Read a book about her life, if you'd like to know more.

When you're at the end
of your rope, tie a knot
and hold on.
-Theodore Roosevelt.

PERSPECTIVE #1:
LIFE IS
FULL OF
OPPORTUNITIES

(DON'T THROW IT ALL IN THE GARBAGE)

CHAPTER 5

Life Is Full Of Opportunities
(Don't Throw It All In The Garbage)

Life gets awfully dark at times. But you don't know what's ahead. Never assume things won't work out well for you. Or you'll be giving up on things you can't see right now.

Perspective #1 is: Life is full of opportunities and we don't want to throw them away.

I KNOW LIFE CAN BE EXTREMELY PAINFUL, BUT HOLD ON

There may be a time to let go, such as during a famine, or if we're injured beyond repair.

But under normal circumstances, we don't want to give up too easily.

When things get really oppressive some press the eject button and end their lives before their time is up.

Life can be super painful. I understand. *But we can't see all we'd miss out on.*

We'd be throwing millions of lost opportunities in the garbage can. Kind of like throwing away millions of dollars, only more valuable.

Once it's too late, though, we'd be looking down at our lives, saying, "Darn, I wasted it. I shouldn't have given up."

INSTEAD OF DOING GOOD WITH OUR LIVES WE LEAVE A BIG HOLE

When we end our lives too soon we don't see in advance all the pain we'll cause. Even in people we barely know.

We lose the chance to do something worthwhile with our lives and instead leave a bunch of people hurting.

So, don't give up.

YOU ONLY GET ONE LIFE TO LIVE

You're going to die soon enough. **Don't rush it.**

Don't jumpstart the process.

There's something worthwhile that can come out of your time here. Don't waste your chance.

IF YOU DON'T FEEL YOU CAN MAKE IT, GO STRAIGHT TO PART TWO FOR HELP

If you're feeling you can't stand the pain any more go straight to part two of this book for strategies. **There are things that can greatly ease that pain and help you through this.**

But then come back and read these chapters, because they can help you for the long term.

Into each life
some rain must fall.
-Henry Wadsworth
Longfellow

PERSPECTIVE #2:
EXPECT LIFE TO HAVE TROUBLE AND IT'LL BE EASIER WHEN IT ARRIVES

CHAPTER 6

Expect Life To Have Trouble
And It'll Be Easier When It Arrives

Life is awful once in a while. I get that.

I don't want to make light of whatever you're going through. **Whatever it is, I know there are times when it just hurts.**

LIFE CAN CUT LIKE A KNIFE SOMETIMES

It can almost feel like a knife cutting inside us it's so painful at times.

These things are real. And none of us is immune to this kind of pain, if we've been here awhile.

I FEEL IT AT TIMES, TOO

I've been there. On a regular basis. **I always get through it but that doesn't mean my head doesn't drop by the weight of it.** Until I get a grip.

In fact, when life is going really well I think, "I bet some kind of trouble is up ahead. Things are going too well."

And you know, I've often been right. **Because pain is part of life here on Earth.** It's like an unwritten law of the Universe.

And that is perspective #2, which tells us that trouble is to be expected. It helps us mentally just to have that in mind, as a bit of protection.

I don't mean like Eeyore, with a woe-is-me attitude.

I'm talking, "Okay, I knew it might come, but I've got this," type of thinking.

If you stick around long enough you'll probably see that good often comes from it all and I'll shed some light on that later on.

But when we're expecting to have trouble it guards us like a mental suit of armor.

Kind of like when someone sneaks up behind us and we scream, because we didn't see them coming. If we know they're there, we won't be taken by surprise, right?

BAD THINGS WILL HAPPEN TO US

So, it helps to be prepared for trouble.

There'll be times when any of these things might happen:

- We'll get sick
- We'll lose a loved one
- Someone will cheat us or let us down
- Things we own will break
- We'll have money issues
- Something we try will fail
- Natural disaster will strike

You name it. Something bad happens to all of us, sooner or later.

LIFE CAN SEEM PERFECT AND THEN TROUBLE COMES

If you've been around very long you've probably had days like these:

You think life is going really well, then all of a sudden you're hit with something that knocks you sideways...

- Maybe you just bought the house of your dreams and then you're told you're going to be laid off.
- Or you get a promotion at work and then your spouse says they wants a divorce.

We need to know it'll be that way once in a while.

It's still going to hurt like the dickens but at least it gives us some breathing room to know that trouble comes to everyone.

TROUBLE CAN HIT US LIKE A TRUCK IF WE'RE EXPECTING LIFE TO BE PERFECT

If we expect life to be a bed of roses we can feel like we've been hit broadside when that trouble finally shows up.

Not to make light of anyone who has actually been in a severe car accident, but sometimes our troubles make us feel like we've been in an emotional car wreck.

There was a time in my life when something really terrible happened and it was like that. I remember telling a friend, "I feel like I've been hit by a truck."

BITTER COMPLAINING IS A SIGN WE WERE EXPECTING TOO MUCH

Some people think life will always go how they want it. Then when a wrench is thrown in their plans they get angry. It's as though they thought life would always go well.

Now, it's okay to talk about our troubles. With the right attitude.

It's a major part of our conversations with each other.

But, if we find ourselves raging mad or terribly depressed when bad comes it means we were expecting life to be perfect. And that's not realistic.

I've done it myself, though, too.

Most of the important
things in the world have
been accomplished by
people who have kept on
trying when there seemed
to be no hope at all.
-Dale Carnegie

PERSPECTIVE #3:

THERE'S MORE TO LIFE THAN WHAT YOU SEE RIGHT NOW

CHAPTER 7

There's More To Life Than
What You See Right Now

Something good may be ahead and we don't even know it.

Perspective #3: There's more to life than what we can see now. *Something good is often right around the corner.*

It helps to know that things are likely to get better.

Eventually.

That can keep us in the game. And that's how the game is won. By patient endurance.

Most great things that have been accomplished looked hopeless for a moment. Even Mother Theresa was told helping people wasn't a good idea when she asked her higher-ups about her plans. But did she give up?

And everyone has times that are a downer. Life is kind of a balance, with its ups and downs.

BAD DAYS DON'T LAST FOREVER

Life can seem rotten, then something happy occurs and life is good again. **So have hope.**

- You could be depressed because the person you're dating hasn't responded to your texts and you saw them with someone else. *Then suddenly you are asked out by a person at work you'd been eyeing for months.*

- Or you're flat broke and feeling like you're going to sink. *Then you get a check in the mail.*

It isn't always that simple, but you get the picture.

IF WE THINK LIFE WILL ALWAYS BE TERRIBLE WE'LL LOSE HOPE

Sometimes people expect life to be awful forever.

If we're expecting the worst we could give up. **Even though things might look better the next morning.** And those who give up have no idea how much is ahead that they're losing.

And even if things get more difficult, rather than better, there are things we can do to make the most of it. **Because there are still opportunities to do something worthwhile, in the middle of our troubles.**

IT'S OKAY TO HAVE FEELINGS WHEN BAD THINGS HAPPEN

You have permission to have feelings, though, okay?

I'm not saying, "Don't feel sad when things are difficult."

Nor am I saying, "Don't be happy when times are good."

What I am trying to get across is **"Remember, life has a way of getting better. In time, anyhow."**

TRUST THERE IS MORE THAN YOU SEE RIGHT NOW

Point being, *you can't trust your eyes.*

Bad days probably won't last forever.

Although, I have to say there are terrible things that can happen that have no remedy. But some people who have been through the hardest of times have made something good come out it.

And, even when they last a long time, there'll still be good moments.

So, just like you have to expect trouble will come, be sure to expect better times to come as well. Eventually.

While there's life,
there's hope.
-Marcus Tullius Cicero

PERSPECTIVE #4:

MOST DAYS HAVE LITTLE 'HELPS' ALONG THE WAY

(WATCH FOR THEM)

CHAPTER 8

Most Days Have Little 'Helps' Along The Way (Watch For Them)

Solutions can take a long time, but when they do come it's like a woman who just had a baby. She's so overwhelmed with happiness over this new child that she forgets all about the pain.

But, in the meantime, what if there aren't any full-blown solutions in sight? **Well, there are almost always some 'breathers' that come our way.** Often on a daily basis.

Breathers are those little moments when something encouraging happens that gives us hope and keep us going. You can call them that because they give you a moment to catch your breath.

If you string together enough breathers you can make it through just about anything.

So, here is Perspective #4: *Expect to find some little 'helps' along the way.*

WHEN WE WATCH FOR RELIEF WE'RE LESS LIKELY TO MISS IT

The funny thing is, the more you expect there to be little moments of relief the more often they come.

Good thoughts are like a magnet, in a way.

Maybe it just means we're more aware, so we notice the things that were already there. **In any case, it's a good practice to expect little signs of hope here and there, so look for them.**

And if it takes a whole lot of little moments of relief just to get us through, then so be it. As long as we get through.

There is value hidden
in every problem:
Don't waste it.
-Dr. Jacinta Mpalyenkana,
Ph.D., MBA

PERSPECTIVE #5:
THERE'S A LESSON IN EVERYTHING

(ALMOST)

CHAPTER 9

There's A Lesson In Everything (Almost)

Perspective #5 is: *Look for lessons all around you.*

Problems come for a variety of reasons, but one is to teach us something we couldn't comprehend any other way.

"WHAT CAN I LEARN FROM MY TROUBLES?"

When you have troubles it's good to ask yourself, "What can I get out of this?"

Because if we don't learn the first time, we often have to repeat the grade. Double ouch.

YOU CAN FIND LESSONS IN ALMOST ANYTHING, IF YOU LOOK

Besides the lessons in our troubles we can learn lessons from:

- Nature
- Little clips of music we're listening to
- The front page of the newspaper (when you read between the lines)
- Bits of conversations we overhear
- The faults we notice in others (What not to do ourselves)

In fact, if you look for it there's a lesson in darned near everything, even the ring around your toilet bowl.

MY TOILET BOWL HAD SOMETHING TO TEACH ME

When you see a ring in your toilet, you haven't cleaned it in a while. Now you have a difficult stain to get rid of.

Some things need to be dealt with right away. On a regular basis. Our relationships are like that.

We need to be quick to say sorry when we've done something that upsets our partner, our children, or whoever. **If we let too much time pass and ignore the problem, resentments build up and it gets harder to resolve.**

Just like the ring around that bowl.

I HAD A LESSON FROM AN ANT INFESTATION

Okay, one more example from just the other day...

We have this sugar ant problem around our house. I don't know why, exactly. I even had an entire ant colony living in my alarm clock, of all places.

The other day, however, I found ants swarming all over my bag of food...

BUT THIS TIME ANTS WERE ON EVERTHING EXCEPT MY FOOD

Normally there'd be ants over everything, including my food. But this time ants were everywhere but my food.

None on my bread. None on my peanut butter jar. None in my granola. Not even any on my tiny box of raisins.

WHY WEREN'T THERE ANTS ON MY FOOD THIS ONE TIME?

The ants had never left me alone like that before. My conclusion? I decided it was a lesson.

WHAT I LEARNED FROM THE ANTS

The ants taught me that it's possible to be safe and protected in the middle of a bad situation, thank God. That's what I picked up from it, anyway.

A bit zany, but I get comfort from it.

PERSPECTIVE #6:
IF YOUR TROUBLES ARE SMALL BE HAPPY THEY AREN'T WORSE

CHAPTER 10

If Your Troubles Are Small Be Happy They Aren't Worse

Sometimes we are bothered by problems that are relatively small. **And Perspective #6 is to, well... keep our troubles in perspective.**

"WOULD I TRADE THESE TROUBLES FOR OTHER ONES?"

Unless we're having the worst of troubles, it's good to be happy with the ones we have.

Everybody has one trouble or other. A fact of life at this present time.

Remember that when troubles come along. And ask yourself if you'd want to trade your problems for something worse. Because it often could be a lot worse.

OUR TROUBLES GET US LOOKING UP

Now, if you're one of my friends who believes we become compost after this life, don't mind me. We'll just agree to disagree.

But I'm always reminding myself there won't be all these troubles in the afterlife. Sigh. (I sigh an awful lot.) If I'm wrong (I trust I'm not), then, oh well, at least it kept me a little happier while here.

We must be willing to let go of the life we have planned, so as to have the life that is waiting for us.
-E. M. Forster

PERSPECTIVE #7:

WHEN ONE DOOR IS CLOSED ANOTHER IS OPENED

CHAPTER 11

When One Door Is Closed Another Is Opened

Here is Perspective #7 for you... *When life closes the door in your face, find the open window.*

We make all kinds of plans for ourselves, but life has a way of putting a wrench in our plans.

My husband is always saying, "Life is what happens when you're making other plans." It's a quote by John Lennon. But my husband says it so often I feel like he came up with it.

Regardless, anyone who has dreams or plans has run into this at one time or another... what looks like a dead end.

But don't give up there.

THINK OF PROBLEMS AS OPPORTUNITIES

We can think of our setbacks as opportunities.

Or, like the song by Bob Marley says, "When one door is closed, another is opened." We might just be getting redirected a bit.

I get the door shut in my face all the time. It frustrates me to no end, but I keep looking for new avenues.

SOMETIMES ROADBLOCKS MEAN, "THIS ISN'T THE BEST ROUTE FOR YOUR LIFE"

I have had the greatest plans. Or so I thought. I got a no, but kept pushing. And still no.

Eventually I do give up and move on to the next plan. With the assumption that, "This just must not be the best thing for my life right now."

And sometimes, in hindsight, I can see why it wasn't for the best. Like when I wanted to go into the Airbnb market, right before the Coronavirus hit.

ASK YOURSELF WHERE LIFE COULD BE DIRECTING YOU

When you get hit with a "No," you might feel depressed for a moment. **But, lift up your head and ask, "Where could this trouble be leading me?"**

Open your mind to new possibilities.

Don't just get stuck there. Some give up when that door shuts in their face. But there's almost always another path you can take. You just have to look for it.

Look and you'll find.

Remember this the next time you hit a roadblock, okay?

Some people bear three kinds of trouble - the ones they've had, the ones they have, and the ones they expect to have.
-H. G. Wells

PERSPECTIVE #8:

ONLY WORRY ABOUT TODAY'S TROUBLES

CHAPTER 12

Only Worry About Today's Troubles

The title says it all. So, I'll keep it short.

Perspective #7... *If it isn't happening right now, don't stress about it.*

You can worry about it later, if it ever comes to pass. No need to add it to your worries today.

There are millions of things that could go wrong, and we can't get anxious about all of them, right? So, let's try to let some of our worries go.

Today has enough trouble. Let's stick to that.

It's a more reasonable load to carry.

Can you do that, friend?

As a saying by Erma Bombeck goes, "Worry is like a rocking chair. It gives you something to do, but never gets you anywhere."

Keeping this in mind will hopefully help you reduce the anxiety you feel.

DO PREPARE FOR THE FUTURE, THOUGH

It's smart to have insurance, keep emergency supplies in your car, give your family contact locations in case of a disaster, etc.

And I think everyone should stock up on food and water. **(I always recommend people buy a little extra non-perishable food when they can, just in case.)**

I'm all for having a plan B.

Just feel good when you've done what you can do. And don't worry about the rest.

I know that can be easier said than done.

WAYS TO LET GO OF YOUR ANXIETIES...

Personally, because I trust there's Someone out there in the universe watching over me I can let go once I've asked for help. **If that doesn't suit you, though, you might**

try writing your troubles down and then burying them, burning them, or throwing them away.

I've heard of people sending them away on a balloon, but I wouldn't want my troubles to land in someone else's yard. They might take it as a bad omen.

Courage is being scared to death... and saddling up anyway.
-John Wayne

PERSPECTIVE # 9:
FACE YOUR FEARS

CHAPTER 13

Face Your Fears

This chapter may be one of the hardest things for some to do. But if you feel sick inside with anxieties, it can help you feel peace right in the middle of a storm.

Perspective #8 is to face your fears. It's like the last chapter, except this is something that's somewhat likely to happen. A looming threat.

IF I'M GOING TO DIE, I'M GOING TO DIE

A long time ago a lady named Esther was brave enough to speak up for some people about to be killed, even though she could be put to death herself. She stared death in the face…

She said, "If I'm going to die, I'm going to die."

There are things that actually might happen, but we don't have control over.

A lot of us these days face the very real threat of running out of money. **And many of us are afraid we, or a loved one, might get sick and die from a terrible virus.**

Others are afraid they'll be made fun of, or looked down upon, for standing up for what's right. (We'll look closer on how to face down some of those common fears in a minute.)

WHAT GOOD DOES IT DO TO BE SCARED?

You may have legit fears, but what good will it do to get anxious about it?

When you're feeling anxious about situations that are threatening there are two keys to eliminating that anxiety:

1. **Look straight at your fears and ask, "What's the worst thing that could happen?"**

2. See if you can accept that possibility. **Can you resign yourself to the thought that this might actually happen?**

If you can face your fears and accept them, you may be able to find peace.

"Okay, so maybe I will die… I can live with that."

A little light, but that's the idea.

ACCEPT WHAT YOU CAN'T CHANGE

Do whatever you can to avoid trouble. Within reason.

But after you've done what you can do, if it's going to happen, it's going to happen. **Why not feel at peace, rather than worry yourself sick?** Kind of a challenging thought. And like I said, you might have a hard time with this one.

But, whoever you are, stare those fears down until you have peace, because feeling anxious about those threats will only make you miserable. When you could be feeling calm inside.

TAKE ACTION IF COVID IS THREATENING TO UNDO YOU FINANCIALLY

We don't have total control here, but there are things we can do to make it better for ourselves financially.

If we keep our head in the sand, and wait for the unemployment check to run out, we'll end up worse off. So, we need to find ways to save money, and earn more.

I've written a book, called 'Stay Afloat Post-CV', and it covers all kinds of ways to make your financial situation a little more secure. **But, regardless, make a plan to cut back on your spending or add to your income, and then act on it.**

DEATH IS EASIER TO ACCEPT WHEN…

I find it easier not to fear dying knowing that hundreds of thousands who've been resuscitated say about the same thing: they see Jesus as a bright light and feel loved and at peace like you can't imagine.

(Some have negative experiences, but we don't want to talk about that. Except to say that sending up a little apology for mistakes squares that away.)

But everyone has the freedom to choose their own beliefs, and for those who aren't of that mindset, death can be a very scary thing.

COVID HAS MANY SCARED THEY MIGHT DIE

If we want to avoid terrible sicknesses there are some limited things we can try. **We can focus on things like eating well, exercising and getting enough sleep to strengthen our immune systems.** Plus, whatever else we can do to try our best to be healthy.

And we can keep in mind that not always, but often the people who die from viruses are not only immune-compromised, but are near death to begin with.

I work with elderly patients, and many wonder, "When will I finally get to die?" Their bodies can't function anymore, their minds don't work properly, they've had a good long life, and they're ready to go.

Of course, death also comes to those who aren't ready. The thing is, we can only control what we can control. **So we do our best, and then try not to worry.**

Doing nothing for others is the undoing of ourselves.
-Horace Mann

CHAPTER 14

The Main Reason We Have Troubles

There's a reason why life is so painful: We are free to make choices, and, unfortunately, some of us choose to be selfish.

All of us start out that way. You know how selfish a kid can be. Everything is "Me, me".

And selfish adults hurt other people. Financially, sexually, through violence, you name it. They want "Something for me…" Even at another person's expense.

So, we people cause almost all the pain in the world.

We cause ourselves pain, too, by our own bad choices. A bad diet, sitting around all day, drinking too much, you know.

SOONER OR LATER IT CATCHES UP WITH YOU…

There's a kind of 'divine karma' in the Universe. **It catches up with us sooner or later.**

We can choose to be selfish and hurt people, but it's gonna come back to us.

And most people who hurt others are just blind. They don't see that by being selfish they're making their lives a mess. **To hate them misses the point.**

I feel sorry for them, because they're wasting their chance to do something good with their life. And if they don't turn it around before it's too late, they'll die with a bad name.

THE MEANING OF LIFE…

People who've died and been resuscitated often say they were shown the movie of their life in fast motion.

(If you want to check out some of them, look on YouTube. Just keep scrolling until you see a person who looks trustworthy, then see what they have to say.)

In the books documenting these cases many say they got a little 'review' and were told to go back and 'love'.

LET'S DON'T MISS THE MAIN POINT… TO LOVE

Now, I hope none of you get all hung up about whether or not people had veritable experiences and miss the *whole point.*

The point is… The best thing we can do with our lives is to love other people.

That's what it's all about.

It's about love.

Being nice and doing things for others. And trying to encourage other people to be loving, too.

That right there gives us a reason for living. And it's a lot more satisfying than anything we could do for ourselves.

Sounds simplistic, but how many people miss it, and waste their time on a bunch of stuff that doesn't really matter?

As I walked out the door toward the gate that would lead to my freedom, I knew if I didn't leave my bitterness and hatred behind, I'd still be in prison.
-Nelson Mandela

CHAPTER 15

A Lack Of Forgiveness Eats Us Up Inside

Now, we all want freedom to choose in life. But when someone abuses their freedom and hurts us, one of the hardest things in the world to do is to forgive them. **But when we hold something against someone it hurts us.** It eats us up.

Whoever did wrong to us only saw from their perspective, not ours.

Feeling hatred towards them doesn't do us any good. The best thing is to forgive.

It doesn't mean it was okay. And it doesn't mean we forget.

But letting go frees us to actually heal.

Think back. Is there anyone who has hurt you? Have you forgiven them?

YOU DON'T HAVE TO 'FEEL' FORGIVENESS TO CHOOSE TO FORGIVE

Even some Holocaust victims have forgiven their prison guards. They made a decision in their heart to forgive, although some didn't feel it at first. **But, somehow the simple act of saying inside, "I forgive them," changes you in time.**

IF YOU'VE DONE SOMETHING WRONG CLEAR THE SLATE

We've all done something or other that's not nice...

- Gossiped
- Told a lie
- Ignored someone who needed help
- Held a grudge
- Looked down on others
- Bragged about ourselves
- Talked in a rude voice
- Been impatient
- Broken a rule
- Taken advantage of someone for sex
- Cheated or stolen

- Been selfish
- Blamed someone else for problems we brought on ourselves

Knowing deep down we've done something wrong, but hiding our head in the sand can make us feel anxious.

It's good to clear the slate, to have a clean conscience and healthier relationships.

CLEAR THE SLATE BY SAYING YOU'RE SORRY

When I was growing up we all got mad and didn't speak for days until we cooled off. If ever.

Then I married into a family that always said, "Sorry," when they did something wrong. That one word makes all the difference in the world.

WE'VE ALL DONE SOMETHING…

Whether you're Buddhist, Hindu, Atheist, New Age, Muslim, Christian, or whatever, we've all done something.

This may not be where you're at, but every day I try to clear my slate above. I say, "Jesus, please forgive me for all the things I've done wrong."

That takes away all my anxiety, because I know the door will be wide open when I get to heaven.

EVERYONE HAS THE RIGHT TO THEIR OWN OPINIONS

You might have different opinions. That's everyone's choice.

But, just to cover your bases, I suggest taking a minute every day to clear that slate anyhow, because I say, "Better safe than sorry."

Whatever you believe, eternity is something important to think about. And, frankly, it's pretty hard to find peace without the belief that someday there'll be an end to suffering.

SANE STRATEGIES TO HELP YOU HANG IN THERE

My grandmother started walking five miles a day when she was sixty. She's ninety-seven now, and we don't know where the heck she is.
-Ellen DeGeneres

EXERCISE IS YOUR HAPPY DRUG

CHAPTER 16

Exercise Is Your Happy Drug

There are a lot of important things to do to help us feel better, but here's the first. Exercise will bring your anxiety and depression down ten notches.

XANAX OR A GAME OF BASKETBALL WITH YOUR KIDS EVERY DAY?

You can take an anti-depression medication every day to right your 'chemical imbalances'. Or you can get off your bum and get physical exercise.

Now, if you need that pill, you need it. Work with your doctor on this.

But see if getting out there and working your lungs daily and getting your cheeks rosy doesn't turn your body chemistry upside down.

It's hard to feel depressed when you've finished heavy exercise. Not impossible, but much less likely.

Now, when was the last time you broke a sweat? Or got rosy cheeks from working out?

If today, great. If it's been a while, though, just up and do it. Even just do a tiny, little thing, okay, honey?

(Those tiny things, when you do them every day, add up to some big changes.)

WHAT GOOD CAN EXERCISE DO?

Why exercise?

- Exercise reduces our stress levels.
- **It produces endorphins, which make you happier.**
- You'll get in shape. It changes how you look, slowly but surely. And that'll make you feel better about yourself.
- You'll give yourself kudos every day because you up and did it.

I have a lot to say about how to get in shape, because I went from 190 pounds down to about 135. So much so that I wrote a weight loss book about it. But you can fit exercise into your life, no matter who you are. **Keep in mind, though, that there are exercises you can do at your desk, watching TV, even while you're eating your lunch, so anyone can get the habit.**

So, get on those tennis shoes and just do something.

TRICK YOURSELF INTO THE EXERCISE HABIT

Be sly about it. Get yourself exercising daily without your brain objecting. Otherwise you'll talk yourself out of it. Here are some no-fail methods to get in the habit:

- Start small. **Commit to a teeny tiny walk or jog around the block or the nearest high school track.** (Just go to the mailbox, if that's too far.)

- **Whatever you choose, do it *every day*.** (You'll miss some days. That's okay.)

- Plop an exercise bike in front of that TV. The time passes quickly that way.

- **HERE'S THE BIGGIE... Make it a law: I can't _____ (eat lunch, watch TV, etc.), until I do my exercise.**

- **Hey, even give yourself a candy bar afterwards, if you want and if that'll get you to do it.** I don't care. Whatever works. "I can have a Snickers bar if I go for my walk." Even walking to the mini-mart each day to buy that candy bar is an accomplishment.

- Maybe power-walk the last 100 feet home, to get your blood pumping. (Your body will give you credit, just as though you'd done it the whole way.)

PLAY SPORTS WITH SOME KIDS AND DO GOOD FOR BOTH OF YOU

Do something active with kids. Play soccer, basketball, foursquare, tetherball, badminton, you name it. You'll feel better.

And so will they. Kids are under a lot of emotional stress these days, and it'll really help if they get that exercise, as well.

This might encourage you... When I was pregnant I played basketball every day with my 9 year old son. And voila! When the baby came out, I kid you not, I looked better than ever.

Gained the weight right back, though, because I stopped playing. Didn't want my baby to get hit in the head with a basketball.

TO GET YOUR CHEEKS ROSY MAKE A LITTLE BIT OF IT BRISK

Try to do a little tiny bit extra to get that blood going. Like jog the last half block of your walk. Do some speed walking. Or go up some stairs. Wear a backpack. Ride that bike a little faster for a minute.

You get the idea.

Don't kill yourself, though. **Take it easy if you feel chest pains, joint pain, or anything else that doesn't seem right.** Check with your doctor.

HOLD YOURSELF ACCOUNTABLE TO SOMEONE OR KEEP SOME KIND OF RECORD

If you have someone cheering you on, that's great. Tell a friend. Post on FB. (You might get others on a good track, too.) Or make notes on your calendar or your phone.

One person caring about
another represents life's
greatest value.
-Jim Rohn

TALK TO SOMEONE WHO UNDERSTANDS WHEN IT FEELS HEAVY

CHAPTER 17

Talk To Someone Who Understands When It Feels Heavy

Having someone you can talk to can help lift the weight off your chest. One time it felt like an iron boot was weighing down on me. I called a friend and it seemed like that weight was lifted. It was amazing the relief I felt.

THERE IS SOMEONE WHO CARES ABOUT YOU

We all have someone who cares about us. Even if they have a hard time showing it. And there's almost always someone we can find who'll listen to our troubles.

KEEP LOOKING UNTIL YOU FIND SOMEONE WHO IS A GOOD LISTENER

Unfortunately, some people are not very good listeners. Myself included, at times. I'm always happy to help, but tend to want to fix the problems.

Other people get overwhelmed. Or just don't get where you're coming from.

It might be hard to come up with somebody who will listen and actually care. **But try until you find someone.**

You can ask friends, family, someone from whatever group you belong to, anyone who gets what you're going through. You can talk to a school counselor, or try praying (if that's your thing), or set up an appointment with a therapist.

Heck, one latch-key kid even used to call the operator each day to check in, back in the day when dialing zero would get you a real live person. She was one of those people who cares for others, and you know, I bet she even looked forward to his calls.

"WHAT IF I'M TOO MUCH OF A BURDEN?"

This is one of those lies we tell ourselves that keep us from getting the help we need.

The truth is, you are not a burden. **You're a person with troubles, just like all the rest of us.**

There are some people who get too freaked-out by other people's problems. If you make the mistake of choosing one of them to talk to, just chalk it up to experience, and try someone else.

Many people, however, actually feel good to be helping. It gives us a purpose in life.

IF YOU'RE FEELING DESPERATE CALL A HOTLINE

Call the crisis line if you're feeling you can't take it anymore and need someone right away.

The National Suicide Prevention line is 1-800-273-8255.

WITHOUT A SOCIAL NETWORK IT MIGHT BE HARDER TO FIND A LISTENER

If you have a social network, and belong to some kind of group, you might be able to find a good listener. But if you aren't involved in any groups, think, "Out of all the people I know, who seems like they care?"

If we're all quarantined, try talking over the phone.

And if it takes a while to find the right person, there's something you might want to try in the meantime...

I can shake off everything as I write, my sorrows disappear, my courage is reborn.
-Anne Frank

WRITING DOWN OUR TROUBLES CAN HELP US THROUGH TOUGH TIMES

CHAPTER 18

Writing Down Our Troubles Can Help Us Through Tough Times

Whether or not you talk to another person, it's helpful to write your problems in a journal. Or wherever.

When we write down our troubles they can feel a lot smaller. Sometimes we even see solutions by the time we're done.

HERE'S THE MOST EFFECTIVE WAY TO HELP

When writing try to:

- Keep the focus as positive as possible.

- Do some problem solving. **Don't just say what's wrong, but also put down what you might try to do to make things better.**

- Be honest. Even if someone might see it later.

So, if there isn't anyone you can talk to, or if you're the John Wayne type... or if you just want something extra that's therapeutic, try writing down your thoughts.

It can still take some of the weight off and help you de-stress.

Because sometimes we just have to be our own best friend.

Meditation: Because some answers can only be found on the inner net.
-Shira Tamir

PRACTICE MEDITATION, MINDFULNESS, OR GUIDED IMAGERY

CHAPTER 19

Practice Mediation, Mindfulness, Or Guided Imagery

Sometimes, when we're stressed we just need to breath deep. There are also some meditation-type practices that can bring us calm and reduce anxiety. Using any one of these techniques should help your stress levels go down measurably.

MEDITATION

In meditation you empty your mind of all the things that are getting you down. You try to focus on absolutely nothing. Which I find very difficult to do.

For some people, though, who are plagued by troubling thoughts, it might be a good way to put the brakes on.

Finding a peaceful spot with few distractions is key. Then sit quietly for several minutes to try and unwind.

MINDFULNESS

The idea here is to fill your mind with thoughts of what is happening in the present, in order to relax and ground you.

- Take 10 minutes or so and sit peacefully.
- Keep your mind on the present moment.
- Try not to think about the past or worry about the future.
- **Be aware of what is going on around you right now, in the moment.**
- Notice your breathing, how you feel, what you hear and what you see.

You can be 'mindful' any time, not just when you're sitting still. You can even be mindful when you're talking to someone, by focusing on what they're saying right now rather than what you plan to say in return.

GUIDED IMAGERY IS A RELAXING SORT OF MEDITATION

Change the first sentence to: The type of guided imagery I'm talking about is a script that helps you picture yourself in a peaceful place.

Some people like to imagine they're on a white, sandy beach. Others, maybe, in front of a mountain lake, or in a log cabin during a rainstorm. Whatever place seems the most comforting to you.

It takes about 10 minutes a day.

You can think of scenarios yourself, but there are some great guided imagery videos on YouTube you might like.

Give it a try and see if it works for you. It can be super relaxing.

A busy mind is full of thoughts, a blissful mind is full of ideas.
-Amit Kalantri

CHAPTER 20

Have An 'Idea Time' To Come Up With Solutions To Your Problems

Yes, some problems aren't easy to solve. But there's usually *something* constructive you can do to help. **And you'll feel a lot less anxious if you have a plan to solve your problems and are working on them.**

It's helpful to have a regular 'Idea Time' or problem solving session. This is a type of focusing I do regularly.

Almost every day there's some problem that threatens to do me in. And I'm super busy, so I use times like when I'm stuck in traffic or am waiting around to have that problem solving session.

I ask myself, **"What problem do I need to focus on right now?"** And I just start brainstorming. Usually there are some breakthroughs that give me hope and a plan of action.

What problems do you need to work on?

Try having an 'idea time' and open your mind up to solving your problems. Instead of just avoiding them and feeling miserable.

Try this:

- Sit quietly. Or do something that doesn't take any concentration.
- Eliminate distractions.
- **Have a focus for the day.** "Today I'm going to focus on new ideas to solve_____."

- Have an open mind. Ideas should come in that you might not have thought of if you weren't focusing.

WE CAN'T FIX EVERYTHING, BUT LET'S FIX WHAT WE CAN

We won't be able to solve all our problems, but we can almost always make improvements. And you might be surprised at all the ideas that come when you take that time to focus on solutions.

The purpose of life is not to be happy. It is to be useful, to be honorable, to be compassionate, to have it make some difference that you have lived and lived well.
-Ralph Waldo Emerson

CHAPTER 21

Get Out Of Yourself For A Bit By Helping Others

This may seem a little off the wall, but doing something good for someone else can help more than you might expect.

It makes us feel better when we're doing something meaningful to help another person.

THERE'S NO LIMIT TO THE GOOD YOU CAN DO

There are unlimited possibilities but just to throw some out there for you:

- Ask a homeless person what they need and buy them something at the grocery store.

- Mow the lawn for the lady down the street whose husband passed away.

- Get some hotdogs for the BBQ and invite someone over.

- Make cookies and bring some to your new neighbors.

- Take a packet of easy to sprout flower seeds and sow them as you walk. Like in 'Miss Rumphius' (a children's book I loved reading to my kids).

- Buy a bag of burgers at Jack in the Box and hand them out downtown, if it feels safe. (Take your kids along. Mine love doing this.)

- Pick up garbage in a public place.

- **Paint uplifting signs and put them along the roadside.** You might get flack for this, but just so you know... anytime you do something worthwhile somebody will try to stand in your way. Just take it as confirmation you're doing the right thing. Remember, like I said, even Mother Theresa was told her idea was terrible.

- **Put cool quotes up around your house.** They'll make you feel a little better and inspire others who see them. I have words all over my house. I get flack for that, too, but oh, well.

  I have a sister-in-law, (who I think must be the nicest person in the world), and she had these tiny, fortune-cookie sized quotes on her window. I'd see them every time I went there, and almost have them memorized. And you know, I still think about them at random times.

It's funny, but even something little like that can influence a person in a good way.

- **Smile, if nothing else.** I know I feel happier when somebody smiles at me. Especially when everything seems wrong with the world. You never know where someone is at inside. Maybe a smile isn't going to change someone's life, but it's better than nothing. They might be glad to know there's one person in the world on their side.

- **Ask people how they are doing.** And really listen. Plus, offer to help if there's even some small thing you can do.

If you want to be happy, set a goal that commands your thoughts, liberates your energy, and inspires your hopes.
-Andrew Carnegie

CHAPTER 22

Set Goals To Give You Motivation For Living

Goals give us purpose. **This step is the most important thing to help you want to get up in the morning.**

For one short time I had no goals. All I could do was count the tiny bumps on my ceiling. The whole day I either slept or sat around.

Most of the time, though, I have pages of goals. I can't wait to wake up each day and get started on them.

Goals keep you going and give you something to look forward to.

DO YOU MAKE RESOLUTIONS AND NOT KEEP THEM? TRY THIS...

Ever made New Year's Resolutions and nothing happened? **Here's how to make sure you actually accomplish your goals:**

- Write down the steps, even the small ones. (Email so-and-so, make this phone call, mail letter, pay for permits, sign-up online...)

- **Make a 'Pay to Play' rule, like I mentioned regarding exercise: "I have to _____, before I can _____."** You decide what... maybe no TV, social media, or video games. Check a thing or two off your list and then you're free to go.

Helps me. The endless number of goals I've made throughout my life almost always get done. And yours will, too, if you take little actions every day.

GOALS THAT MAKE YOUR CORNER OF THE WORLD BETTER MOTIVATE MOST

Some goals are personal. Like losing weight or saving money for a car. That's great.

Any goals are motivating. **But they're especially motivating if they involve making life a little better for others in your corner of the world.**

It gives you a reason for being here.

If your goals are related to doing something for someone else, that'll inspire you the most.

You don't have to change the world, though. Make any goals you want. You can think about bigger goals later on.

Get off the track of doubt and gloom, get on the sunshine track – there's room.
-Anonymous

CHAPTER 23

Sunshine... Another 'Happy Drug'

Sunshine improves your mood. And that can help you fight off depression.

Sunshine can also help you:

- Sleep better

- Lose weight

- Have more energy

- Get rid of skin problems

- Have stronger teeth and bones

- Reduce your chances of getting diabetes, cancer, heart disease, and even the flu

Yes, we're told sun exposure causes skin cancer. But you can still get Vitamin D if you wear sunscreen. **And sunshine is the best way to get Vitamin D.** It's the natural way.

Just don't overdo it. Maybe 10 minutes a side?

I avoid sun on my face like the plague. But lately I've been hiding in the yard to sunbathe. Won't work in the winter where I live, but that's how it goes.

If you're able, see if you feel better after some time in the sun... you'll be getting all the other benefits, as well.

And for the wintertime, here's something else that helps...

Look deep into nature, and then you will understand everything better.
-Albert Einstein

CHAPTER 24

Spend Time In Nature

There's benefit to getting outdoors, even when the sun's not shining. Being in nature can be grounding.

It's good for your soul to put your feet in the sand, to hear the birds, to see plants, trees, flowers, and so much more.

Nature is a reminder that some things are still right in the world. And there's more where that came from.

So, spend time in a park, at a beach, in the woods, or anywhere in nature, because you'll see the goodness and beauty, and know that not everything is rotten right now.

Our food should be our medicine and our medicine should be our food.
-Hippocrates

CHAPTER 25

Flood Your Body With Nutrition To Help Your Body's Chemistry

Here's another important way to adjust your body's chemistry.

Anti-depressants and other pharmaceuticals all have side effects, one of which is increased risk of suicide. Maybe because taking a darned pill doesn't do enough to solve our problems. (But again, check with your doctor before going off any medication, in case you really have to have them. But then work on improvements in your life and see if your doctor will agree to adapting the plan. One thing at a time.)

SO, WHAT COLOR IS YOUR FOOD?

Every time you eat, look at your plate. Do you see all shades of white and brown?

If so, expect to have problems, because you need color to keep your body and mind healthy. So, eat the rainbow and flood your body with nutrition.

Try to fill your plate half-full of fruit and vegetables. Like mom said, "You've got to eat those vegetables!"

Just try, okay? If you even make an effort, that's great.

A SMOOTHIE IS A GREAT WAY TO GET COLOR IN YOUR DIET

One super simple way to get color in your diet is to make a smoothie.

Banana. Frozen berries. Cover with water. Blend well.

(Too sour? You may have unripe berries. Add more bananas. Or use apple juice instead of water, if that suits you better. My kids like to add milk in theirs.)

YOU CAN BOOST THE SMOOTHIE ONCE YOU'RE IN THE HABIT

Once you're in the habit try adding spinach or other dark leafy greens. Or add superfood powder.

Some powders I like are:

- **Moringa leaf powder** (Possibly the most nutritious food in the world)

- **Chlorella or Spirulina** (These two are loaded with micronutrients)

- **Wheat grass powder** (Some say wheat grass juice can cure just about anything. Fresh is better, but this is the next best thing)

- **Red beet powder** (The iron in it builds your blood and oxygenates it)

Anyhow, try your best to cut back on junk and fill up on nutritious food. It'll do your body and your mind good.

The amount of
sleep required by the
average person is
five minutes more.
-Wilson Mizener

CHAPTER 26

A Good Night's Sleep Keeps You In Better Spirits

We all know a good night's sleep affects your mood. Think how cranky kids get when they're tired. We grown-ups are wired the same way.

Do you get at least eight hours most every night?

Life's troubles feel a lot worse when we're short on sleep. If you're not getting enough, here's another solution to help ease your feelings of depression and anxiety.

Lack of sleep also causes health problems. And being unhealthy makes depression worse, too.

THERE ARE THINGS YOU CAN DO TO HELP CURE INSOMNIA

1. **Being in sunshine or just being outdoors helps you sleep better.** I remember my son used to conk out after a day of sun at the pool. His head would tip over into his spaghetti, while he was in his highchair, and he'd be out like a light.

2. **Hard work outdoors helps, too.** People who do hard work outside often sleep soundly. Exercising outdoors is awesome, too.

3. **Listen to nature sounds on YouTube when you're trying to fall asleep.** You can listen to the sound of rain, thunder, waves on the beach and probably more. It can really be relaxing, so give it a try.

4. **Watch what you eat and drink.**

    •   **Avoiding chocolate, soda, coffee, and of course, energy drinks about seven hours before bed is smart.** Having caffeine too late can keep many people awake till morning. Sometimes you might beat the algorithm, like when you're exhausted. But often it'll catch you and keep you lying there with your eyes wide open.

        I can't prove it, but I would guess that almost all people who say they have insomnia at night are just getting too much caffeine after noon.

        One of my kids often can't fall asleep until morning hours. He drinks soda every night. When I pointed it out he said, "Oh, no, it's not the soda. I just have insomnia."

- **If you have acid reflux you've probably noticed certain foods just don't mix well with lying down.**

- **Drinking too much liquid at night can make you have to get up to use the bathroom.** Then, who knows if you'll fall back asleep right away.

Now, if worse comes to worse and you really can't fall asleep, the best thing to do is to lie down anyhow, feet up and eyes closed, and listen to a podcast or something. That'll keep your active brain satisfied, but let the rest of your body relax.

But try these strategies first and see if you can get a better night's sleep.

I drink too much. The last time I gave a urine sample it had an olive in it.
-Rodney Dangerfield

CHAPTER 27

Alcohol (And Some Substances) Can Make Life Feel 10X Worse

I almost never drink, but have no problem with someone drinking a glass or two of alcohol.

When we have more than that our problems tend to get worse. Even though most do it to forget their problems.

At one New Year's Eve party, as a teen, my photograph was in a modeling ad on the coffee table. I noticed someone had drawn a mustache on my face. Because I was flat-faced that left me bawling in their back room, feeling like it was the end of the world.

The problem would've hardly fazed me if I were sober.

If you over-imbibe I'm sure you have your own stories.

IF YOU NEED HELP GETTING CONTROL

See if you can have just one or two, and then switch over to something non-alcoholic.

And if that doesn't work...

I know people who quit drinking with AA and made some good friends, who don't drink. I also know people who've never been to a single meeting and say how terrible AA is.

Sometimes we reject the best thing for us. Something to keep in mind, if it's too hard to stop after just one or two drinks. (Okay, maybe three, but don't you lose track after that?)

Sometimes having fun with your best friend is all the therapy you need.
-Anonymous

CHAPTER 28

Find Distractions When You Need To Get Your Mind Off Your Troubles

Sometimes, when life really hurts we just need to get our mind off our troubles. Especially if we've tried everything else.

This is something you probably already do, but now you can feel good about it, because, "I'm taking care of myself."

Some common distractions that can help you make it through a stormy time in your life are:

- **Hanging out with friends**

  There's almost nothing more fun than to spend time with your buddies, hanging out and having a good time. Especially if you like doing the same things.

  It can get out of hand if there's too much alcohol, or drugs involved, though, so hopefully you can navigate that.

  And, yes, it is possible to still feel very alone, even in a crowd of people. Give it a try, but sometimes we need a whole lot more.

- **TV or movies**

  I watched a movie so depressing once I literally wouldn't watch another one for 20 years. (Other than kids' shows, like Swiss Family Robinson.)

  You can probably handle it, but still, choose something inspiring. So it brings you up, not further down.

- **Web-surfing**

  This can be educational, which builds you up. Or entertaining, which lifts you up (potentially).

  Definitely helps pass the time. In fact, sometimes it seems we end up in a time warp, while surfing. "Where did all the time go?"

- **Music**

    If you make your own music this is an awesome, creative way to distract yourself.

    And if you can create music with some kind of positive message, whether political, social or whatever, it can be super powerful. This is something you can really feel good about.

    And then, I want to suggest something... Listen to the song, 'Dancing in the Moonlight', and try to imagine what I see:

    All of us, after the troubles of this life are over, having a party together in the 'good life' that never ends, and dancing to this song.

    Things will be better then, and not only that, but we'll understand just why life here was so dang difficult in the first place.

- **Do art**

    If you're artistic you can lose yourself for hours working on a picture or painting. **And, again, you can create something with a positive message that adds something good to the world in some tiny way.**

    Maybe even a mural.

    And if you're not that creative, you can get yourself an adult coloring book. There are supposedly tons of them available online, which seems to say something about all of our stress levels.

    We're feeling it. And as some have found out, getting immersed in some kind of coloring page can reduce that stress.

- **Hobbies**

    Whether you're into fixing cars, knitting, wood working, photography, or any other hobby, it can help you get your mind off your problems for a while.

    And there's almost always some way to up it a level and make something out of it that rocks the world a bit.

    Think photography that educates people about some issue. Or fixing cars for someone unable to afford taking their car to the shop. Knitting blankets for babies born addicted to drugs. You get the idea.

- **Board games**

  Some I like are Trivial Pursuit, which I'm terrible at, the Ungame, Mastermind, and chess (though I haven't played it much more than a handful of times), but you probably have your own favorites.

- **Shopping**

  There can be something constructive about finding something new to wear, to decorate your house with, or to make life easier somehow.

  Careful, though, or you'll add to your stress when you run low on money. Maybe try St. Vincent de Paul's where you can get clothes for $1.95 each or some other type of bargain hunting.

Life is a 'you-know-what' at times, and sometimes we just need something else to focus on.

So, if you're feeling awful and need to just make it through the day, don't be hard on yourself. **Find something to do that'll help you forget your problems for a little while.** These activities can help us hold on and make us feel happier.

CHAPTER 29

A Note About Panic Attacks

I've known people who've had them and they sound really scary. Some describe it as feeling like you can't breathe and worries sort of take you over.

I'm not an expert on panic attacks. But if you've ever had one and are afraid you may have another, I'll share what little I know.

I heard a licensed counselor say most people get through them fine, even though they feel they're going to die. If you have one tell yourself, "This is scary, but I will most likely be fine."

Call 911, if you do feel it's life threatening.

Try something grounding to help snap you out of it:

- Eat or drink something healthy, right away, if you're able.
- **Call a friend or tell someone what is happening.**
- Sing (preferably something with good lyrics).
- I'd pray, but that may not be where you're at.
- Do some quick physical exercises to get your blood going better, if possible.

What you *don't* want to do is just sit there, do nothing, and think, "I'm afraid I'm going to die right now." Hopefully if you take some kind of action you'll be able to ride through it a little easier.

And, this may not apply to you, but just food for thought: I know at least two people who made a connection between their panic attacks and some substances they were using. It caused them to quit and that ended up being a good thing.

Post note: after writing this I did experience a suffocating sort of panic attack and I'll give a glimpse of what happened to me... I prayed. "Jesus forgive me my sins and help me, and yada, yada," but nothing. Then I started telling myself, "God is good. He's going to help me... etc." and it gently faded away. Thought I ought to share that, for those of you who're open to the more spiritual side of life.

CHAPTER 30

12 Things To Do When Someone You Care About Is Feeling Suicidal

There are no easy, one size fits all answers. But here are 12 things you can try.

1. If you don't think they'll actually commit suicide, ask yourself, "What if I'm wrong?" **Treat the situation as serious. The National Suicide Prevention line is 1-800-273-8255.** Look on your phone for local numbers also. **Call 911 if it's an emergency.**

2. **Let them vent.** They feel like no one cares. Show them you do by listening.

3. **Don't judge or tell them their faults.** Now is not the time.

4. **You can ask questions that come to mind like, "Is there anything you think would help this situation?"** Can get them thinking on a more positive track.

5. **This is delicate, but you can ask them, "Is there anything going well in your life right now?"** It helps when we see our cup half full. Some will feel better when they focus on the good things, but others are so down they'll think you're callous for asking.

6. **Try to get them to go for a walk with you.** Or play sports or do some kind of vigorous exercise. It almost always makes us feel a bit happier. You have to do it every day, for it to last, but anything helps.

7. **Help them brainstorm solutions to their problems.** "What's the worst problem you're dealing with right now?" Offer your help. Maybe they have money issues, and you could take them to the food bank. Or help fix their car, etc. Whatever it may be.

8. **Be careful about 'telling' them what to do to solve their problems.** But you might be able ask, "Do you think x, y, z would help the situation?"

9. **Give them something to look forward to.** "Can I have you over for lunch tomorrow?" Or "I'll call you when I get home, okay?" Then do it. You might help them to hang on one more day this way, when they're going through a difficult time.

10. **Try to get them in counseling, if they're willing.** All the same, there's no substitute for a friend or loved one who will listen. They realize the counselor is getting paid.

11. **Check in on them daily, or even hourly.** It helps immensely to know someone is there for you.

12. Send an encouraging text or note to cheer them up when you're not there, to remind them you care.

Final Note From The Author

COME VISIT ME AT MY WEBSITE

Come visit me at my website, where you can enter fun contests, sign up for a free short consultation, get freebies, find life changing content and more: **jillandyou.com**

HOPING THE BEST FOR YOU

I am hoping things will go well for you. I realize we could be in for some rocky times post-Coronavirus days, but let's make the most of the opportunities we have, so long as we're able.

It's hard to say how tough it'll be for us, but hang in there and always hope for brighter days.

Life is difficult, but precious, so take care of yourself.

You matter.

All the best to you.

-Jill

Author Bio

Jill is the author of 'The Whole Life Makeover Series", among other books, all designed to help you make the most of your life.

She and her baker husband, Paul, have a boatload of bio, step, adoptive and foster kids. Eight they've raised start to finish, more or less. And at least twelve in total, (depending on how you count).

The Guy Upstairs inspired her to start the non-profit, Inspiration 2 Go, which helps people in impoverished countries with mini-job projects and basic necessities.

You can visit her at her main website:
jillandyou.com

The doable way to get the body you want

THE

TRANSFORM

YOUR

BODY

DIET

Right: Younger Jill, who weighed up to 190 lbs. Below: Age 56, a healthier Jill weighing under 135 lbs.

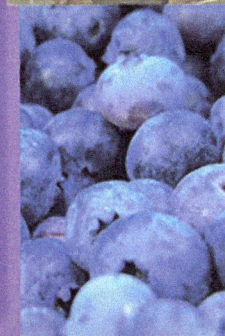

AKA: The 14 Step, Exercise
To Fit Your Life,
Trade Fat For Muscle,
Boost That Metabolism,
Do Better Than Keto, Flood
Your Body With Nutrition
And Still Indulge Once
In A While Diet

JILL BEYTEBIERE

From 'THE WHOLE LIFE MAKEOVER SERIES'

BOOKS FROM 'THE WHOLE LIFE MAKEOVER SERIES':

THE TRANSFORM YOUR BODY DIET: AKA: The 14 Step, Exercise To Fit Your Life, Trade Fat For Muscle, Boost That Metabolism, Do Better Than Keto, Flood Your Body With Nutrition And Still Indulge Once In A While Diet

The Transform Your Body Diet will give you keys to help you do what you never could before.

You'll be able to:

- **Fit in exercise even if you have no time**
- **Eat the foods you love**
- **Forget about counting calories**
- **Boost your metabolism**
- **Eat superfoods for extra energy**
- **Break your sugar addiction (And still eat sweets occasionally)**
- **Learn about intermittent fasting**
- **Learn why Keto is not a long term solution**
- **Make simple recipes that are nutritious and quick**

Jill used to weigh 190 pounds and has kept over 50 pounds off now for almost a decade.

The steps she shares are backed by scientific studies, common sense, and practical experience. And they are in your reach.

Coming soon.

You can look for it at Jill's website:

jillandyou.com

Enter there, for a limited time, to win a free copy of one of Jill's books. (Winner every weekend when contest is running.)

Will be available on Amazon. You can also ask for it at Barnes and Noble or from your local library.

STAY AFLOAT POST-CV

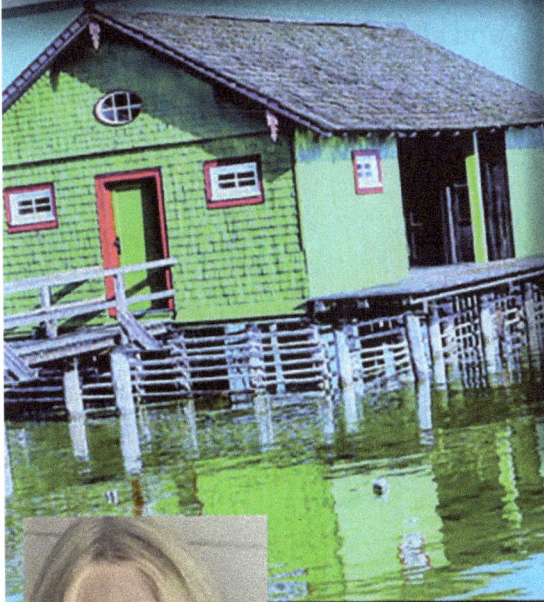

Stretch Your Dollar From Here ToTimbuktu, Find A Side Hustle, Own A Home Free And Clear, Invest In The Best, And Still Have Money To Give Away (If All The Stars Line Up)

JILL BEYTEBIERE

From 'THE WHOLE LIFE MAKEOVER SERIES'

STAY AFLOAT POST-CV: Stretch Your Dollar From Here To Timbuktu, Find A Side Hustle, Own A Home Free And Clear, Invest In The Best, And Still Have Money To Give (If The Stars All Line Up)

Everyone wants more money... but this book can help you:

- **Make the very most of what you already have, even if it's tiddlywinks.**

- **Scrounge up more income, where once there was none.**

- **Be richer than you ever imagined, when it comes to things that really matter.**

You'll learn, also, how Jill's large family, while cash-poor, and embarrassingly having to rely on the food bank some of those years, was able to pay off their mortgage in very short time. (On mainly a single-earner, barely above minimum wage income.) Twice.

Because like dummies, once they got out of debt, they decided to take out an even bigger loan, and were almost sunk, if it weren't for...

Well, get the book, and maybe, if things work out in your favor, you'll be able to pay off your mortgage, too, in record time... and all that other good stuff.

Coming soon.

You can look for it at Jill's website:
jillandyou.com

Enter there, for a limited time, to win a free ebook copy. (Winner every weekend when contest is running.)

Will be available on Amazon. Or ask for it at Barnes and Noble or your local library.

A toolbox full of helpful 'people' tips

RELATIONSHIP

RX

How To Develop Relationships Post-Covid, Reach The Hearts Of Your Loved Ones, Deal With Them When They're Impossible, And Dig Yourself Out Of The Doghouse When You've Messed Up (From Someone Who Has Done Some Digging)

JILL BEYTEBIERE

From 'THE WHOLE LIFE MAKEOVER SERIES'

109

RELATIONSHIP Rx: How To Develop Relationships Post-Covid, Reach The Hearts Of Your Loved Ones, Deal With Them When They're Being Impossible, And Dig Yourself Out Of The Doghouse When You've Messed Up (From Someone Who Has Done Some Digging)

Do you sit alone in your house, wishing you had more people in your life? Or do you have people in your life, but find them impossible to get along with?

Would you like to learn how to turn things around, either way? **We all need some strategies to get relationships going, as well as keep them from falling apart.**

Jill and her husband have been through the teenage years with ten of their children (step, adoptive, fostered and bio), which has been fun overall, but a bit of a 'school of hard knocks'. The author, though an imperfect parent, will share with you some lessons learned along the way.

And getting along with anyone is almost an art. If one type of solution doesn't do it, you need to try another, until something works. **This book has a list of strategies, to help you improve every type of relationship you're in.**

Jill will admit it's not easy. Her marriage, for one, sometimes feels like it hangs on by a string of "I'm sorry's," though she loves the guy dearly. **But the tactics here help her keep things together, and will hopefully be useful for you, as well.**

The day Jill gives up trying these things is the day she'll have to pull this book out of print. Because not many relationships hold on by accident.

And this little manual can help you, too, so you don't become an island of one. **If you implement these ideas it can, hopefully, help you avoid the pitfalls that sink a lot of relationships.**

Look for it soon at Barnes and Noble, on Amazon, at your local library, or at the author's website: jillandyou.com.

BRAND YOUR LIFE'S WORK

How To Make Your Dream Business, Create An Online Presence, Do It Local, Nail It With Your Copy, Advertise The Heck Out Of It, And Scale It To The Highest Heavens (*Disclaimer Included)

JILL BEYTEBIERE

From 'THE WHOLE LIFE MAKEOVER SERIES'

BRAND YOUR LIFE'S WORK: How To Make Your Dream Business, Create An Online Presence, Do It Local, Nail It With Your Copy, Advertise The Heck Out Of It, And Scale It To The Highest Heavens (*Disclaimer Inside)

Are you looking to start up a new business? Or makeover the one you have? **Some say over 90% of new businesses fail, and if you would like to up your chances of succeeding, this unlikely stay-at-home mother has some suggestions to share, (for whatever they're worth).**

Never in a million years would Jill have thought she'd be studying marketing and business. But in the course of figuring out how to sell her books, she's acquired an education and a half, admittedly mostly through listening to thousands of YouTube tutorials and Podcasts.

Who says you have to go to a four year University to learn this stuff?

An information junkie, Jill loves the commercials, too, and has signed up for almost every free webinar known to man... *or a lot,* anyhow. When YouTube offers a family plan with no ads, she asks herself, *"Now, why in the world would I want that?" Seriously.*

As someone who's crazy for new ideas, she comes up with some brilliant hair-brained marketing schemes, while doing mindless things like vacuuming. Though she admits, they have yet to be tested.

Copy. Copy. Copy. And advertising tips to the yin yang. She's got you covered.

All this to say, if you want everything distilled down, saving yourself countless hours of time, plus ideas galore and her own take on things, however ridiculous, you can hardly stand to miss this book.

Coming soon. Will be available on Amazon. Ask for it at Barnes and Noble or from your local library.

You can also buy it at Jill's website. Enter there to Win a free copy of one of Jill's books. (Winner every weekend): jillandyou.com

A Life Plan Makeover Guide For Young And Old

LIFE
TO THE
FULLEST

The Ultimate Guide To Help
You Design The Best Life
Possible, Find Your Life's
Work, Do Something
With It Online, Fit In
Travel, And More

JILL BEYTEBIERE

From 'THE WHOLE LIFE MAKEOVER SERIES'

LIFE TO THE FULLEST: The Ultimate Guide To Help You Design The Best Life Possible, Find Your Life's Work, Do Something With It Online, Fit In Travel, And More

This book about living life to the fullest sells you on the idea of making the very most out of your life and taking action to make your dreams a reality.

It covers a lot of crucial ground, including how to:

- **Have a great but sane sex life**

- **Accomplish your goals**

- **Fit in travel**

- **Enjoy people and keep your relationships intact (even when they're being impossible)**

- **Find your life's work**

- **Develop your own online presence**

This book was written for young people just about to set out on life, but the information can apply to all of us.

Coming soon. Will be available on Amazon. Ask for it at Barnes and Noble or from your local library.

You can also buy it at Jill's website. Enter there to Win a free copy of one of Jill's books. (Winner every weekend): jillandyou.com

Get more done in a day than humanly possible (almost)

EXPLODE

YOUR

LIMITS

Time Management Strategies To Get You Beyond The Daily Grind, Help You Squeeze The Most Out Of Life, And Enable You To Accomplish Your Dreams

JILL BEYTEBIERE

From 'THE WHOLE LIFE MAKEOVER SERIES'

EXPLODE YOUR LIMITS: Time Management Strategies To Get You Beyond The Daily Grind, Help You Squeeze The Most Out Of Life, And Enable You To Accomplish Your Dreams

Do you want to get the absolute most out of your life but are bogged down by the daily grind? Then you need this inspiring and strategic guide. **It'll take your life from ordinary to extraordinary and help you accomplish more than seems humanly possible.**

There are tips and strategies to help you:

- Tame the clutter monster
- Get a college equivalent education (and become indispensable to your boss) while brushing your teeth
- Hatch brilliant plans during your downtime
- Layer activities to get exponentially more done with your time
- Fit in exercise no matter how busy you are
- Multiply what you get done in the kitchen
- Make the most of time with your kids
- Use your Ecto-Brain (your phone) to keep your days running smoothly
- Keep your house a little better than presentable, without a maid
- Plus tons of other valuable tips and insights

The methods here can help you accomplish a lifetime's worth of goals in a year's time. Over the course of a year these strategies helped the author develop numerous websites, write several books, start three online businesses (though now defunct), study Spanish, French, Hebrew and Kreyol, travel almost monthly, get an education in subjects such as marketing, ecommerce, graphic design, public speaking and video editing, start Inspiration 2 Go, (a nonprofit helping people in impoverished countries)... and so much more.

All while working full-time and keeping tabs on a houseful of seven teenagers, plus a grandbaby.

Jill learned that in order to contribute more to this planet than just clean dishes and laundry, you have to be creative and think outside the box.

She didn't want to just raise her kids to raise their kids, ad infinitum, but rather to make some kind of difference in the world and teach her kids to do the same.

Would you, too, like to do more than just survive? Do you want to accomplish things you now only dream about doing? **When you put these novel time management strategies into action you'll see outstanding things happen and will increase your effectiveness exponentially.**

Don't waste another day settling for mediocre. Your life may be only half of what it could be without it.

Coming soon. Will be available on Amazon. Ask for it at Barnes and Noble or from your local library.

You can also buy it at Jill's website, where you can enter to win a free copy of one of Jill's books. (Winner every weekend, for a limited time): jillandyou.com

www.ingramcontent.com/pod-product-compliance
Lightning Source LLC
Chambersburg PA
CBHW062009090426
42811CB00005B/797